U0065809

慈悲篇
智慧法語

愛心、關懷、拔苦

心道

第二輯

The way of Mind II :
Words of wisdom

Compassion:
Love, Caring, and Freedom
from Suffering

心道法師 語錄
By Dharma
Master Hsin Tao

目錄

Contents

作者簡介

心道法師一九四八年生，祖籍雲南，幼失依怙，為滇緬邊境孤雛。十三歲隨孤軍撤移來台，十五歲初聞觀音菩薩聖號，有感於觀音菩薩的悲願，以「悟性報觀音」、「吾不成佛誓不休」、「真如度眾生」刺身供佛，立誓徹悟真理，救度苦難。

　　二十五歲出家後，頭陀行腳歷十餘年，前後在台北外雙溪、宜蘭礁溪圓明寺、莿仔崙墳塔、龍潭公墓和員山周舉人廢墟，體驗世間最幽隱不堪的「塚間修」，矢志修證，了脫生死，覺悟本來。

生道場」，展開弘法度
生的佛行事業，為現代
人擘劃成佛地圖。為了
推動宗教共存共榮，法
師以慈悲的華嚴理念奔
走國際，並於二〇〇一
年十一月成立世界宗教
博物館，致力於各種不
同宗教的對話，提昇對
所有宗教的寬容、尊重

Compassion: Love,
Caring, and Freedom
from Suffering

慈悲篇

智慧法語

愛心、關懷、拔苦

滿足。這些年來，心道
法師以禪的攝心觀照為
本、教育弘法為主軸，
用慈悲願力守護人類心
靈，以世界和平為終生
職志，帶領大眾實踐利
益眾生的宏大願力，祈
願佛陀法脈永傳不息，
讓佛法真諦普傳後世。

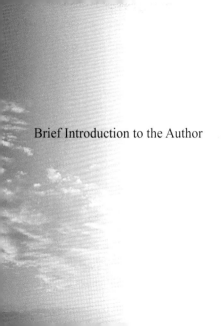

Brief Introduction to the Author

Born in upper
Myanmar in 1948
to ethnic Chinese
parents of Yunnan
Province, Master Hsin
Tao was left orphaned
and impoverished
at an early age.
Having been taken
in by the remnants of

Compassion: Love,
Caring, and Freedom
from Suffering

慈悲篇
智慧法語

愛心、關懷、拔苦

ROC military units operating along the border of Yunnan, China, he was brought to Taiwan in 1961 when he was 13. At the age of 15, he was deeply moved by the compassion of Guanyin Bodhisattva

Compassion: Love,
Caring, and Freedom
from Suffering

慈悲篇
智慧法語

愛心、關懷、拔苦

of Guanyin," "I
will never rest
until Buddhahood
is attained," and
"Liberating all
beings by living in
Suchness."

After becoming a
Buddhist monk at the
age of 25 and making

a vow to attain
enlightenment, Master
Hsin Tao traveled on
foot for over ten years,
practicing austerities
in lonely and secluded
locations, including
Waishuangxi in
Taipei, Yuanming
Temple in Yilan,

Compassion: Love,
Caring, and Freedom
from Suffering

智慧法語

慈悲篇

愛心、關懷、拔苦

Chingtzulun Grave
Tower, Longtan
Cemetery, and the
ruins of the first-
degree Scholar Chou
in Yuanshan, Yilan
county.

Having arrived at
the Fahua Cave on
Fulong Mountain in

early 1983, Master Hsin Tao undertook a fast which was to last over two years, during which time he attained deep insight into the meaning of "Only when all beings are liberated, is enlightenment fully

Compassion: Love,
Caring, and Freedom
from Suffering

慈悲篇
智慧法語

愛心、關懷、拔苦

attained." Standing
on the summit of the
Ling Jiou Mountain,
looking down at
the Pacific Ocean,
Master Hsin Tao felt
great compassion for
the suffering of all
sentient beings. After
his solitary retreat

In addition, Master Hsin Tao strived hard to gain international support with the compassionate spirit of the Buddhist Avatamsaka Vision (of the interconnectedness of all beings in the universe), and

Compassion: Love,
Caring, and Freedom
from Suffering

慈悲篇
智慧法語

愛心、關懷、拔苦

of world peace and a
promoting awareness
of our global family
for love and peace
through interreligious
dialogues. The spirit
of MWR is enshrined
in the words "Respect,
Tolerance, and Love."

The ideal of Chan

lives through the
spirit of "Prajñā" or
Enlightened Wisdom.
And he hopes for
them to practice
Buddha's teachings
unceasingly, and learn
to stop clinging, so
that tranquility and
contentment of mind

Through compassion,
he makes great
efforts to protect and
care for all sentient
beings. Taking the
establishment of world
peace as his lifelong
commitment, he leads
people to work for
the great cause of

benefiting all sentient
beings, ceaselessly
helping them achieve
liberating truth through
Dharma practice for
generations to come.

心之道 智慧法語（第二輯）
慈悲篇-愛心、關懷、拔苦

The Way of Mind II:
Words of wisdom
Compassion :
Love, Caring, and Freedom
from Suffering

「慈悲」就是常替別人想，
別人就會替你想。

Compassion: Love,
Caring, and Freedom
from Suffering

慈悲篇
智慧法語

愛心、關懷、拔苦

Compassion means
always thinking about
the needs of others;
doing so, you will find
that others do the
same for you.

大悲心
是對眾生慈愛的心，
對任何的事事物物、
有情無情都要有慈悲，
都不要傷害。

Compassion: Love,
Caring, and Freedom
from Suffering

慈悲篇
智慧法語

愛心、關懷、拔苦

With a mind of great
compassion, you treat
all sentient beings
with loving kindness.
Regard all beings
and all things with
a mind of compassion
and refrain from
harming others.

在工作中，人與人之間
常常會發生衝突，
這就是考驗修行的時候，
我們要很有包容力，
要能尊重別人，
也要有愛心。

Interpersonal conflict is
inevitable at work; take
such situations as a test of
your practice, especially
your capacity to genuinely
respect others and face
difficulties with patience
and an open heart.

常以慈、悲、喜、捨
四無量心
去面對生命中的緣，
人人都會關懷你、幫助你
不論到哪裡
都會有非常好的緣。

When we approach all
situations in life with the
four sublime attidudes—
loving kindness,
compassion, sympathetic
joy, and equanimity—we
find that others are caring,
kind, and helpful, such
that we feel welcome
wherever we go.

要怎麼樣耕耘慈悲？
把禪修中所證得的智慧，
以慈悲無我的心供養
給眾生，使人人得到無礙的
生命解脫力量。

How does one cultivate compassion? You use the wisdom and selflessness cultivated through meditation to help others surmount obstacles and tread the path of awakening.

要去利益他人，
首先要降伏自己的心，
包容一切是非、
善惡、好壞，
學習心如虛空。

Compassion: Love,
Caring, and Freedom
from Suffering

慈悲篇
智慧法語

愛心、關懷、拔苦

In order to truly benefit
others, you have to
begin by taming your
own mind so that it
becomes spacious and
free from the tyranny
of such dualities as
right and wrong,
good and bad.

Compassion: Love,
Caring, and Freedom
from Suffering

慈悲篇
智慧法語
愛心、關懷、拔苦

Compassion softens
the heart and mind,
allowing one's innate
wisdom to manifest
and come into
full play.

如何轉禍成福？
就是在日常生活裡行善。

Compassion: Love,
Caring, and Freedom
from Suffering

慈悲篇

智慧法語

愛心、關懷、拔苦

How can misfortune
be transformed into
good fortune? By
practicing virtue
in daily life.

只要一切是為了利益
眾生，去做就對了。

Compassion: Love,
Caring, and Freedom
from Suffering

慈悲篇

智慧法語

愛心、關懷、拔苦

When your motivation
is to benefit all sentient
beings, the results are
bound to be good.

尊重、包容
以及慈悲大愛，
是對治苦難
與衝突的良方。

Compassion: Love,
Caring, and Freedom
from Suffering

慈悲篇
智慧法語

愛心、關懷、拔苦

Respect, tolerance,
love, and great
compassion are
effective remedies for
dealing with conflict
and tribulation.

有佛法的思想，
就能承擔該來的痛苦，
坦然地安住在心性上。

Compassion: Love,
Caring, and Freedom
from Suffering

慈悲篇

智慧法語

愛心、關懷、拔苦

Firmly grounded in
the perspective of
the Buddha-dharma,
we approach all the
difficulties of life
with a cool and
composed mind.

隨時隨地導引念頭
去利益眾生，
時時刻刻都不忘失眾生，
這就是菩提心。

Compassion: Love,
Caring, and Freedom
from Suffering

慈悲篇

智慧法語

愛心、關懷、拔苦

Directing every
thought to benefiting
all sentient beings—
this is bodhicitta.

找出生命健康的法則，
就是「慈悲喜捨」。

Loving kindness,
compassion,
sympathetic joy, and
equanimity—this is
the secret to health
and happiness.

學佛，就是生生世世
學習發菩提心、
行菩薩道。

Practicing Buddhism
means generating
bodhicitta and treading
the bodhisattva path,
life after life.

少欲無為，
是一種讓身心得到自在
最好的方法。

Reducing one's desires
and letting things take
their natural course—
this is the best way to
mental and physical
well-being.

造福就是要去耕耘福田，
福田在每個眾生心裡。

If you want to reap
happiness, then you have
to cultivate the field of
merit in your heart.

用慈悲
面對我們人生各種的緣。

Compassion: Love,
Caring, and Freedom
from Suffering

慈悲篇

智慧法語

愛心、關懷、拔苦

In each and every situation,
compassion is essential.

轉識成智，
轉惡成善，
轉貪成布施，
轉瞋恨成慈悲，
就是生活的佛法。

Transforming
emotional bias into
wisdom; evil into
goodness; greed into
generosity; hatred
into compassion—this
is how to practice
Buddhism in daily life.

人為什麼會有衝突？
因為彼此之間沒有空間，
彼此擠壓。

Compassion: Love,
Caring, and Freedom
from Suffering

慈悲篇

智慧法語

愛心、關懷、拔苦

Conflict arises due to
narrow-mindedness,
attachment, and a
lack of tolerance.

擴大自己的心量，
成為無所不在的空間，
彼此擁有一份愛的空間，
才能不斷累積善緣。

Compassion: Love,
Caring, and Freedom
from Suffering

慈悲篇

智慧法語

愛心、關懷、拔苦

Caring for others
and expanding one's
breadth of mind until it
becomes conterminous
with space itself—this
is how to continually
accumulate merit.

Compassion: Love,
Caring, and Freedom
from Suffering

慈悲篇

智慧法語

愛心、關懷、拔苦

When you meet
adversity, let go
of biased and
confrontational
attitudes, sincerely
give of oneself, and
use the situation to
practice self-reflection
and compassion.

佛法所追求的
是永恆的生命、
無障礙的智慧，
還有慈悲遍滿的生命。

The goals of Buddhist
practice are the
deathless, unobstructed
wisdom, and an
unlimited capacity
for compassion.

如何結善緣、不結惡緣？
就是要寬宏大量地
去接納一切來到
你面前的緣。

Compassion: Love,
Caring, and Freedom
from Suffering

慈悲篇

智慧法語

愛心、關懷、拔苦

How do you establish
wholesome affinities
with others rather than
unwholesome ones?
By magnanimously
accepting everything
that comes your way.

Compassion is not
something we do for
other people; it's for
oneself. The greater
the compassion, the
greater the benefit.

能夠全心的
為一切眾生出生入死，
在水深火熱裡
與眾生同甘共苦，
就是行菩薩道。

Compassion: Love,
Caring, and Freedom
from Suffering

慈悲篇
智慧法語

愛心、關懷、拔苦

Wholeheartedly
striving to benefit all
sentient beings through
thick or thin, come hell
or high water—this
is how to tread the
bodhisattva path.

Equipped with
acceptance and
forgiveness, the
wise person ranges
far and wide.

「是非」的原則
是將心比心，設身處地的
為他人想一想。
當同樣的行為，
由別人加諸在我身上時，
我會怎麼樣？

When considering
right and wrong,
empathize with others
and reflect on how you
would feel if censured
for the same behavior.

如何在這個世間上
做一個最幸福的人？
就是要過慈悲喜捨的人生

Compassion: Love,
Caring, and Freedom
from Suffering

慈悲篇

智慧法語

愛心、關懷、拔苦

If you want to be
happy, all you have
to do is live a life
grounded in loving
kindness, compassion,
sympathetic joy,
and equanimity.

Putting compassion
into practice gives
rise to happiness
and wisdom.

在工作當中心量要大，
尊重、包容、
博愛每個人，
為社會、世人，
做出一份生命中
值得回味的事情。

Compassion: Love,
Caring, and Freedom
from Suffering

慈悲篇
智慧法語

愛心、關懷、拔苦

At work, you need to have
enough breadth of mind to
accept, respect, and love
others; by doing so,
you will make a
lasting positive
impression on others.

止惡行善
要從哪裡做起呢？
嘴巴講好事，
耳朵聽好事，
不要講是非，
常起慈悲心，
人生才幸福。

Compassion: Love,
Caring, and Freedom
from Suffering

慈悲篇
智慧法語

愛心、關懷、拔苦

Refraining from evil
and doing good is the
way to happiness. You
start by speaking and
listening in a positive
manner, avoiding
gossip, and generating
a compassionate heart.

The Way of Mind II : Words of wisdom

日常生活中
要常能究竟利他，
下一生就會有好的緣。

Compassion: Love,
Caring, and Freedom
from Suffering

慈悲篇
智慧法語
愛心、關懷、拔苦

Practicing altruism
in daily life brings
about favorable
circumstances in
future lives.

工作就是在進口福田，
不要拒絕點點滴滴
造福的機會。

Compassion: Love,
Caring, and Freedom
from Suffering

慈悲篇

智慧法語

愛心、關懷、拔苦

Consider your
workplace as a field
for cultivating merit,
and never miss an
opportunity to
benefit others.

假如在工作中生起煩惱，
就該對自己多下功夫，
不要因為小小的事情
就掛在心頭、悶在心中，
避免讓內心習慣於
累積這些煩惱。

Compassion: Love,
Caring, and Freedom
from Suffering

慈悲篇
智慧法語

愛心、關懷、拔苦

When you find yourself
in a negative emotional
state at work, regard
it as an opportunity to
hone your practice. And
whatever you do, don't
get into the habit of
dwelling on
small problems.

行善不一定要表現出來，
起心動念的善
就會帶給你如意；
同樣地，
起心動念的惡，
也會讓你感到不順利。

When you genuinely practice virtue, you don't feel like you have to make a display of it. When your thoughts are wholesome, you feel like things are going well; when your thoughts are unwholesome, you feel like everything is difficult.

時時刻刻耕耘好福和慧，
把因果做好，
現下的生活就是淨土，
就是福報，就是修行。

Cultivating virtue and
wisdom from moment
to moment, this very
life becomes the
pure land. This is the
practice which leads to
true happiness.

Passing from
life to life, when
your bodhicitta is
sufficiently strong,
all your karmic
obstructions
will vanish.

發菩提心
就是覺悟的心，
行菩薩道
就是把覺悟的種子
再播送出去。

Compassion: Love,
Caring, and Freedom
from Suffering

慈悲篇
智慧法語

愛心、關懷、拔苦

Bodhicitta is the mind
of enlightenment;
treading the
bodhisattva path is a
way of disseminating
the seeds of
enlightenment.

真正的愛心是不退轉、
不褪色的愛心。

有智慧的人生，
就是消化日常生活
所遇到的問題。

Compassion: Love,
Caring, and Freedom
from Suffering

慈悲篇

智慧法語

愛心、關懷、拔苦

Endowed with
wisdom, one is capable
of overcoming each
and every problem
encountered in
daily life.

Compassion: Love,
Caring, and Freedom
from Suffering

慈悲篇
智慧法語

愛心、關懷、拔苦

You know you are
mature in the practice
when you care more
about others than
about yourself.

常常注意自己的時候，
煩惱就多；
多為別人想的時候，
煩惱就少。

Compassion: Love,
Caring, and Freedom
from Suffering

智慧法語

慈悲篇

愛心、關懷、拔苦

Always thinking about
yourself multiplies
your troubles; caring
for others
lessens them.

不管處於善緣或惡緣，
都能作善，
以造得下一生的善緣。

Compassion: Love,
Caring, and Freedom
from Suffering

慈悲篇

智慧法語

愛心、關懷、拔苦

It's possible to
cultivate virtue
in whatever
circumstances we find
ourselves in, good or
bad; this is how to
generate favorable
conditions in a
future life.

生活碰到逆境時，
就是修行的機會，
如果用修行的心面對一切，
做什麼都會很甘願。

Compassion: Love,
Caring, and Freedom
from Suffering

慈悲篇
智慧法語

愛心、關懷、拔苦

When you encounter
adversity, take it as an
opportunity to hone
your practice. Doing
so, you can handle
whatever life happens
to throw at you.

每一個人都能發
「緣起成佛」的菩提心，
讓一切眾生
獲得無量的福祉，
這才是生生世世
享用不盡的快樂。

Compassion: Love,
Caring, and Freedom
from Suffering

慈悲篇
智慧法語

愛心、關懷、拔苦

Everyone has the
capacity to generate
bodhicitta; vowing to
attain buddhahood for
the sake of benefitting all
sentient beings, you enjoy
inexhaustible happiness
from life to life.

Compassion: Love,
Caring, and Freedom
from Suffering

慈悲篇
智慧法語

愛心、關懷、拔苦

What is happiness?
Nothing more than
loving kindness,
compassion,
sympathetic joy,
and equanimity.

我們時刻都要有修養，
都要能包容、
消化一切，
才能再去製造更美好、
創新的果報。

Continually practicing
self-cultivation
and magnanimity,
accepting everything
that comes your way,
you are bound to get
good results.

碰到每一個人的時候，
就是一種緣份，
要知道惜緣、惜福、
種福、造福。

Compassion: Love,
Caring, and Freedom
from Suffering

慈悲篇

智慧法語

愛心、關懷、拔苦

All personal
associations are due to
karmic affinities and
conditions laid down
in past lives; never
miss an opportunity to
establish wholesome
affinities with others.

在眾緣和合當中，
如果能夠生起慈悲心，
就能夠具足愛心、
樂觀、積極、正面。

If you can generate a
mind of compassion
when karmic
conditions come
together, you will face
life with a mind
filled with love
and optimism.

Compassion means
caring; liberation
means letting go.

要打開心志，
勇往直前。
以服務為目的，
以慈悲心為出發點，
去利益眾生。

You have to resolve
to strive forward,
with benefiting others
as your goal, and
compassion as your
point of departure.

Compassion: Love,
Caring, and Freedom
from Suffering

慈悲篇

智慧法語

愛心、關懷、拔苦

As soon as you
generate bodhicitta,
you become a
bodhisattva.

每個人如果只為自己，
福氣就小；
如果能為人人貢獻跟服務
福氣就大。

Compassion: Love,
Caring, and Freedom
from Suffering

慈悲篇

智慧法語

愛心、關懷、拔苦

If you only think of
yourself, then your
happiness is limited;
if you strive to serve
others, then your
happiness is vast.

做的善業不要據為己有，
一定要分享，
當迴向的時候，
就會跟眾生環扣在一起，
功德就會擴大。

Compassion: Love,
Caring, and Freedom
from Suffering

慈悲篇
智慧法語

愛心、關懷、拔苦

When you do a good,
deed don't try to
keep it for yourself;
by sharing the merit
with others you stand
in solidarity with all
sentient beings, and
your virtue grows.

如何讓累生累世的恩怨，
轉換成我們生命的資糧？
就要做「慈悲喜捨」
的工作。

By practicing loving
kindness, compassion,
sympathetic joy, and
equanimity, all the
gratitude and resentment
accumulated in our
previous lives becomes
a resource for awakening
in this life.

心能平等，
就能處於一個和諧的世界；
心若不平等，將永遠
處於不滿、不平、
不合理的世界。

Compassion: Love,
Caring, and Freedom
from Suffering

慈悲篇

智慧法語

愛心、關懷、拔苦

When the mind is
harmonious, we live
in a peaceful world;
when the mind lacks
harmony, we live in a
world of strife
and discontent.

學習佛法
就是學習智慧，
智慧就是
消除內心的罣礙跟迷惑，
解除生死的困擾，
懂得生命的原理，
產生良性的循環。

Compassion: Love,
Caring, and Freedom
from Suffering

智慧法語
慈悲篇

愛心、關懷、拔苦

Practicing Buddhism means
cultivating wisdom. Wisdom
means dissolving the obstacles
and confusion in the heart and
mind; becoming free from the
tribulations of life and death;
understanding the meaning
of life; and entering into a
beneficial cycle.

Vowing to attain buddhahood
begins with generating
bodhicitta; generating bodhicitta
means vowing to guide all
sentient beings to enlightenment;
guiding all sentient beings to
enlightenment means practicing
loving kindness, compassion,
sympathetic joy, and equanimity.

Only with a firm vow,
a pure mind, and
loving kindness is it
possible to eliminate
obstructions and
benefit society. This is
what it means to
make compassion
one's work.

如果能把內心的仇恨，
化為慈悲喜捨，
未來生生世世
都是幸福快樂、
好運好命。

Compassion: Love,
Caring, and Freedom
from Suffering

慈悲篇

智慧法語

愛心、關懷、拔苦

Transforming
hatred into loving
kindness, compassion,
sympathetic joy, and
equanimity, your
future lives are sure to
be happy ones.

If you have money, use
it to do good deeds; if
you don't have money,
cultivate a good heart.

最簡單的賺錢方法，
就是慈悲喜捨；
最簡單得到人緣的方法，
也是慈悲喜捨。

Compassion: Love,
Caring, and Freedom
from Suffering

慈悲篇

智慧法語

愛心、關懷、拔苦

Practicing compassion
and joyful giving is the
simplest way to a life
blessed with wealth and
harmonious interpersonal
relationships.

我們要養成慈悲和智慧，
不去累積煩惱，
不讓無明沉澱內心，
讓生命過得清清爽爽。

Compassion: Love,
Caring, and Freedom
from Suffering

慈悲法語

智慧法語

愛心、關懷、拔苦

Cultivate wisdom and
compassion, and don't
allow defilements
and ignorance to
accumulate in your
heart. Doing so, life is
relaxed and easy.

常常訓練自己的心
柔和、柔軟，
如此人人碰到你都會轉化
為快樂的緣。

Compassion: Love,
Caring, and Freedom
from Suffering

慈悲篇
智慧法語

愛心、關懷、拔苦

Train the mind to be
soft and gentle; this
way you'll get along
well with everyone
you meet.

什麼是生命最好的收穫？
就是廣結善緣，
製造良性循環。

Living a bountiful
life means getting
along well with others
and entering into a
beneficial cycle.

今生要把存入的記憶做好
把覺悟的種子做好，
把善業的種子做好，
生生世世
都要做發願成佛的事情。

In the present life,
sow wholesome
seeds, the seeds of
enlightenment; these
will bear fruit as
you vow to attain
buddhahood in every
future life.

要擁有富足的物質生活，
就要常常做付出、
利他的事情。

If you want to be
prosperous, then
you have to practice
generosity.

自利
就是能夠知因知果，
利他
就是能夠慈悲喜捨。

Understanding the
law of karma, you
benefit yourself;
practicing loving
kindness, compassion,
sympathetic joy,
and equanimity, you
benefit others.

追求佛陀真正的智慧，
發菩提心，傳承度眾，
才是佛乘。

Compassion: Love,
Caring, and Freedom
from Suffering

慈悲篇
智慧法語

愛心、關懷、拔苦

Aspiring to realize the
wisdom of a buddha;
generating bodhicitta;
leading all sentient
beings to liberation—
this is the way
of the buddhas.

學佛的人、行菩薩道，
就是自己不成佛沒有關係
希望每一個人都成佛。

Compassion: Love,
Caring, and Freedom
from Suffering

慈悲篇
智慧法語

愛心、關懷、拔苦

Treading the
bodhisattva path
means guiding others
to buddhahood without
any regard for one's
own enlightenment.

每時每刻，
都能盡形壽、獻生命，
用無盡的生命
來奉獻眾生，
讓眾生離苦得樂，
這樣的人生才有意義。

Dedicating your
body and life to the
benefit of all sentient
beings; taking every
opportunity to help
others be free of
suffering—this is a
meaningful life.

若能視一切眾生
都是我們的親屬，
廣結善緣，就會讓內心
獲得更大的福祉。

Compassion: Love,
Caring, and Freedom
from Suffering

慈悲篇

智慧法語

愛心、關懷、拔苦

Connecting favorably
with others by
regarding all beings as
you kith and kin,
you experience
great happiness.

愛心的資源
就是付出、關懷、濟助。

Giving, care, and
assistance—these are
the resources of love.

有智慧的生活
就是一種和諧的生活。

A life lived wisely is a
harmonious life.

慈悲就是一切
物質生活如意、
順利的緣起。

Compassion: Love,
Caring, and Freedom
from Suffering

慈悲篇

智慧法語

愛心、關懷、拔苦

With compassion, all
things go well.

慈悲就會耐煩，
耐煩也是一種忍辱波羅蜜。

Compassion: Love,
Caring, and Freedom
from Suffering

慈悲篇
智慧法語

愛心、關懷、拔苦

With compassion
comes patience and
perfect forbearance.

學佛的好處，
可以得到自身智慧的提昇。

Buddhist practice
is a way of
cultivating wisdom.

Compassion: Love,
Caring, and Freedom
from Suffering

慈悲篇
智慧法語

愛心、關懷、拔苦

Being a bodhisattva
means helping others
generate bodhicitta.

學佛就是要好好地發心，
來成就利他的精神。

Practicing Buddhism
means vowing to
benefit others.

利他，才是這個世界
真正的核心思想。

Benefitting others is what life is all about.

常常誦持＜大悲咒＞，
便能有效地清除
內心的憂慮，
保持一顆覺醒的心。

Compassion: Love,
Caring, and Freedom
from Suffering

慈悲篇
智慧法語

愛心、關懷、拔苦

Frequently chanting
the Dhāraṇī of Great
Compassion is an
effective way to
eliminate anxiety and
make the mind
more buoyant.

念咒
不只是口頭念誦而已，
而是要知道
如何生起一顆慈悲心，
接引人來造福行善，
消除自身的無明煩惱。

Compassion: Love,
Caring, and Freedom
from Suffering

慈悲篇
智慧法語

愛心、關懷、拔苦

Mantra practice is
more than just reciting
the words; you have
to do it in such a way
that you generate
compassion and
eliminate ignorance
and defilements.

Practice means
continually generating
compassion and
wholesome aspirations.

Compassion takes you
into the world; wisdom
takes you beyond it.

慈悲心與愛心
是一生的原動力，
有此原動力，
則一生沒有一件事
不成功。

Compassion and love
are the driving force of
life; they bring success
at every turn.

Compassion: Love,
Caring, and Freedom
from Suffering

慈悲篇
智慧法語

愛心、關懷、拔苦

A bodhisattva harbors
not even the
slightest thought of
harming others.

慈悲是究竟的解脫。

Compassion is
complete liberation.

一個人如果具足慈悲心，
就是佛的化身。

Anyone with a
mind imbued with
compassion is a
manifestation of
the Buddha.

有智慧的生命，
就不會結惡緣。

Endowed with
wisdom, you never
make enemies.

學佛，
就是讓自己的心地
是慈悲的，
讓自己的處事
是智慧的。

Compassion: Love,
Caring, and Freedom
from Suffering

智慧法語
慈悲篇

愛心、關懷、拔苦

Practicing the way of
the Buddha, your heart
becomes filled with
compassion and you
approach all situations
with wisdom.

Cultivating
wholesome affinities in
your work and service
activities, you plant
the seeds of happiness
and good fortune from
life to life.

Compassion: Love,
Caring, and Freedom
from Suffering

慈悲篇
智慧法語

愛心、關懷、拔苦

A person with clarity
and insight has
mastery over the
mind and cultivates
wholesome affinities.

The Way of Mind I

Words of wisdom
Cultivate Wisdom　Cultivate Mind　Cultivate Spirituality
By Dharma Master Hsin Tao

心道法師法語清新如露，滴入人心之力量正如暮鼓晨鐘，

讓人在煩惱當下豁然開朗，開啟自性明徹的一方天空。

閱讀心道法師語錄，可以讓個人內修自省的功夫，

在日常生活中發酵延續，成就自利利他的菩薩行。

修慧篇

放下執著，
同時也放過自己一馬。
Stop clinging and
give yourself a break !

修心篇

心平安，世界就平安了。
When our mind is at peace,
the world is at peace.

修行篇

修行，就是找回真實的生命。
Spiritual practice is
just living a life of truth.

隨身智慧寶典

第一輯

修慧篇／修心篇／修行篇

心之道

智慧法語　心道法師　語錄

1套3本
珍藏價200元

「深呼吸，合掌，放鬆，寧靜下來，讓心回到原點。」

分禪

釋心道 著

One-minute Meditation

Take a deep breath; put your palms together; relax;
quiet down; let your heart return to its origin

By Dharma Master Hsin Tao

定價250元

　　心道法師自西元二〇〇九年推出一分禪，此可謂平安禪法的一大方便法門。

　　本書特別從心道法師這兩、三年的相關開示中，選出一分禪的原理與實際操作方法中的要訣內容，以供有志禪修者參考。

心之道 智慧法語（第二輯）

慈悲篇-愛心、關懷、拔苦

心道法師語錄

主　　編：洪淑妍
責任編輯：李慧琳
英文審校：石麗君
美術設計：宋明展
發 行 人：歐陽慕親
出版發行：財團法人靈鷲山般若文教基金會附設出版社
地　　址：23444新北市永和區保生路2號21樓
電　　話：(02)2232-1008
傳　　真：(02)2232-1010
網　　址：www.093books.com.tw
讀者信箱：books@ljm.org.tw
法律顧問：永然聯合法律事務所
印　　刷：皇城廣告印刷事業股份有限公司
初版二刷：2013年8月
定　　價：新台幣180元(1套2冊)
I S B N：978-986-6324-41-3

The Way of Mind II : Words of wisdom
Compassion: Love, Caring, and Freedom
from Suffering

Words of Dharma Master Hsin Tao
Editor in Chief: Hong, Shu-yan
Editor in Charge: Li, Huei-lin
English Proofreading:Lisa Shih
Art Editor: Song, Ming-zhan
Publisher: Ouyang, Mu-qin
Published by: the Subsidiary Publishing House of the Ling
Jiou Mountain Prajñā Cultural Education Foundation
Address: 21F., No.2, Baosheng Rd., Yonghe Dist., New
Taipei City 23444, Taiwan (R.O.C.)
Tel: (02)2232-1008
Fax: (02)2232-1010
Website: www.093books.com.tw
E-mail: books@ljm.org.tw
Legal Consultant: Y. R. Lee & Partners Attorneys at Law
Printing: Huang Cheng Printing Company, L
The Second Printing of the First Edition: August 2013
List Price: NT$ 180 dollars(Two-Manual Set)
ISBN: 978-986-6324-41-3

國家圖書館出版品預行編目(CIP)資料

心之道智慧法語. 第二輯 / 洪淑妍主編. -- 初版.
-- 新北市：靈鷲山般若出版, 2012.12
　　冊 ；　公分
ISBN 978-986-6324-41-3(全套：精裝)

1.佛教說法 2.佛教教化法

225.4   101024788